THE REALITIES
OF THE ENDTIME

FREEMAN JOHNSON

Kingdom Publishers

Realities of the Endtime
Copyright© Freeman Johnson Etukakpan

All rights reserved. No part of this book may be reproduced in any form by photocopying or any electronic or mechanical means, including information storage or retrieval systems, without permission in writing from both the copyright owner and the publisher of the book. The right of Freeman Johnson Etukakpan to be identified as the author of this work has been asserted by him in accordance with the Copyright, Designs and Patents Act 1988 and any subsequent amendments thereto.
A catalogue record for this book is available from the British Library.

All Scripture Quotations have been taken from the New International Version and the King James Version of the Bible.

ISBN: 978-1-913247-73-7

1st Edition by Kingdom Publishers
Kingdom Publishers
London, UK.

You can purchase copies of this book from any leading bookstore or email **contact@kingdompublishers.co.uk**

THE REALITIES OF THE ENDTIME
Freeman Johnson

Printed for
Mega Life Network
New Life Covenant Church
Eiswerder Str. 18, 13585 Berlin, Germany
info@newlife-international.com
www.newlife-international.com

CONTENTS

DEDICATION	9
FOREWORD	11
CHAPTER ONE	13
The Endtime Manifestations	13
Rapture, what does It Really Mean?	13
Transformation	14
Transformation of the Dead	15
Carrying Away	16
The Anti-Christ	17
The Beast	18
The Sea	18
The Ten Horns	18
The Dragon	19
The False Prophet	20
CHAPTER TWO	24
The Purposes of Rapture	24
Deliverance of Believers	24
The Wrath of God is for His Enemies;	26
The Transformation of the Living Believers	27
Bringing the Dead in Christ into the Kingdom	28
Reuniting the Living and the Dead in the Kingdom	31

CHAPTER THREE	35
The Period of Rapture	35
1. The Beginning of Sorrows	37
2. The Great Tribulation	39
3. The Second Coming of Jesus Christ	48
4. The Period of Rapture of the Saints	51
CHAPTER FOUR	56
Life After The Rapture: Part 1	56
The Judgmental Wrath	58
Hell, the Lake of Fire	61
The Bottomless Pit	62
CHAPTER FIVE	64
Life After The Rapture: Part 2	64
In Heaven or on Earth	65
CONCLUSION	69

DEDICATION

This book is dedicated to our Lord Jesus Christ, the Saviour and Master of my soul.

My Appreciation goes to one untraceable Mr. Tony whom I met in 1999 in Berlin, and whom the Lord used in teaching me the mystery in the book of Revelation.

I want to thank Bishop Abraham Bediako of Christian Church Outreach Mission, for his efforts in raising generational Christian leaders in Germany; and also Pastor Kingsley Nimo who pastured me for about eighteen years.

My special love and thanks go to my Sweetheart, Pastor Patricia Johnson and our children; Gihon, Saviour, Judah and Havilah for their relentless efforts and support at the root of every given vision in my life. Finally I want to appreciate my leaders, Deacon Bassey Udoh, Deaconess Vivian McIntosh, members of Powerline Prayer Network and every member of Mega Life Family of New Life Covenant Church – You are unique! God bless you.

FOREWORD

Under the dispensation we are now living, the greatest expectation of a believer is the rapture.
Rapture strikes fear in the heart of many, brings joy to some and doubt to the majority who do not understand or are confused about the period in which we live. Years and seasons have gone by and many respected Bible scholars and prophets have written volumes of books concerning the Endtime, but the majority of believers are still ignorant about the time of rapture.

The Realities of the Endtime was written precisely to state in clear and simple form the truths about the mysteries of the rapture and what will happen thereafter. Some of the revelations may be controversial and contrary to the understanding you have learned, preached and even written before. But as true scholars, believers and leaders, reading patiently through the pages of this book will either yield to, or change your understanding concerning your Christian destination.

On the other hand, you will find sufficient information about the prophecies and the revelations of the Bible concerning this topic. It will unfold the great events bringing history to consummation including the revelation of Jesus at His second advent.

The illuminations and ideas that provided the input for this book are purely revelations from the Holy Spirit of the hidden meaning of the ignored truths of the Bible. Personal studies could not have achieved this except through Almighty God who provided a teacher through a supernatural arrangement to teach his servant the basic truth that became the principle source of this important piece of work.

Mr. Tony, a Nigerian, whom I met for only three days in 1999, is the man God used to ignite my understanding of the endtime prophesies.

You cannot afford to ignore the future, especially when the events to come have been prophesied or programmed. You need to understand God's program for the future, and this book will clear your doubts through the power of the Holy Spirit who is the great teacher.

And ye shall know the truth and the truth shall make you free. John 8:32

And they that understand among the people shall instruct many. Daniel 11:33

Like a sailor, having the right compass is vital when taking a journey: you know the destination but not sure of the direction. As a Christian, your compass is the truth in the Word of God; do not accept stories that sound like truth. Search the Scriptures and you shall have understanding of what shall befall the world in a short time. Your understanding will become a source of help to many.

A second major purpose of this book is to reveal and to analyse the timing of each manifestation of the endtime so that Christians may know what to do and what to expect in these last days.

CHAPTER ONE

The Endtime Manifestations

Most of the events or manifestations that draw the attention of every believer and non-believer whenever endtime is mentioned have been collated to form the teachings of this book. Although many are well informed about the Endtime manifestations, the great unanswered questions have always been; "But How?" and "When?" Most of the "Hows" and "Whens" shall be answered logically as we ascend the ladder of time and season through the five chapters of this book.

I shall revolve the Endtime events around one of the major and positive promises which began in the Old Testament - the *Rapture of the Saints*. Within this promise, we are able to understand most of the events that are to take place, their seasons and periods before the end of age.

Rapture, what does It Really Mean?

Let us consider the following Scriptures:

Behold; I show you a mystery; we shall not all sleep, but we shall all be changed. In a moment, in the twinkling of an eye, at the last trump; for the trumpet shall sound, and the dead shall be raised incorruptible, and we shall be changed. 1 Corinthians 15:51-52

For the Lord himself shall descend from heaven with a shout with the voice of the archangel, and with the trump of God: and the dead in Christ shall rise first; Then we which are alive and remain shall be caught up together with them in the clouds to meet the Lord in the air; and so shall we ever be with the Lord. 1 Thessalonians 4:16-17

Immediately after the tribulation of those days shall the sun be darkened, and the moon shall not give her light, and the stars shall fall from heaven and the powers of the heaven shall be shaken. And then shall appear the sign of the son of man in heaven and then shall all the tribes of the earth mourn and they shall see the son of man coming in the clouds of heaven with power and great glory. And he shall send his angels with a great sound of a trumpet, and they shall gather together his elect from the four winds, from one end of heaven to the other. Matthew 24:29-31

From these Scriptures, rapture can be given a definition. It could be defined as the transformation and carrying away of the believers of Jesus, both the dead and the living before the Endtime destruction of the beast (anti Christ), the false prophet, the unbelievers and those that shall receive the mark of the beast.

Transformation

Rapture involves transformation, which Paul described to the Corinthians as the *"mortal putting on immortality"* and *"the corruptible putting on incorruptible"* (1Corinthians 15:53) Metamorphosis and Transfiguration are two similar words that could best explain what this transformation actually implies. Metamorphosis suggests a striking alteration of structure, appearance or circumstances: while transfiguration suggests an immediate, typically exalted or glorifying change. The changes have to do with our human nature, human senses and our natural body.

For this corruptible must put on incorruptible, and this mortal must put on immortality. 1 Corinthians 15:53

What makes the body to be perishable and corruptible shall be overwhelmed and overtaken by the power of the Holy Spirit. The barrier in our sight that prevents us from seeing through the throne of God like Stephen in the book of Acts will be removed.

But Stephen, full of the Holy Spirit, looked up to heaven and saw the glory of God, and Jesus standing at the right hand of God. "Look," he said, "I see heaven open and the Son of Man standing at the right hand of God." Acts 7:55-56 (NIV)

The bodyweight that cannot overcome the gravitational force will be withdrawn. And lastly, our inability to understand in full, shall forever be swallowed up. If the same spirit that raised Jesus Christ from the dead dwells in us, He shall quickened our mortal and corruptible body to be changed. We shall be changed to possess the characteristics of the Son of man at his ascension to heaven and that of Elijah at his flight in a chariot of fire. There may be no alterations in our physical appearances for we know that we shall be like Him when he appears.

Dear friends, now we are children of God, and what we will be has not yet been made known. But we know that when Christ appears, we shall be like him, for we shall see him as he is." 1 John 3:2 (NIV)

Transformation of the Dead

Apart from the transformation of the living, rapture also involves the transformation of the dead in Christ Jesus.

In a moment, in the twinkling of an eye, at the last trump: for the trumpet shall sound, and the dead shall be raised incorruptible, and we shall be changed. 1 Corinthians 15:5

Paul, in this letter, did not only assure us of the resurrection of the dead during rapture but also their transformation. At the sound of the last trumpet, the transformation of the dead saints will occur at supersonic speed. In a moment, in the time an eye will take to blink or in a fraction of a second, the process of transforming millions upon millions of saints will be complete. In other words, the souls of the saints shall be called up to appear before the Lord.

In death, the present body ceases to exist; rather it decays. The soul becomes the body to the spirit. At rapture, therefore, the dead saints with their souls and spirit will be called up to the Lord. The first body would be dropped forever.

Now this I say, brethren, that flesh and blood cannot inherit the kingdom of God; neither doth corruption inherit incorruption. 1 Corinthians 15:50.

It is only the soul that can inherit the Kingdom of God because it can regenerate and it is heavenly in nature. Hence, the living saints who have been transformed shall meet the souls of the saints who have dropped the earthly body through death. And they shall together, meet the Lord and the angels in the air.

Carrying Away

After the transformation of the believers (both the living and the dead), they shall be carried away, made to change position, hidden from the ordinary sight of men and shall meet the Lord in the air. As it is written in the Scriptures:

And he shall send his angels with a great sound of the trumpet and they shall gather together his elect from the four winds from one end of heaven to the other. Matthew 24:31

The saints shall be gathered by the angels to meet the Lord. For the Lord shall descend from heaven to take his own to himself. And when we meet the Lord, we shall be like him and shall be with him forever.

Beloved, now are we the children of God, and it doth not yet appear what we shall be, but we know that, when he shall appear, we shall be like Him, for we shall see Him as He is. 1 John 3:2

Now, we have been sanctified, created anew, so we are the children of God. But the natural body remains the same. After we are transformed and are carried away, it is not revealed what we shall be.

For there is a natural body, and there is also a spiritual body. 1 Corinthians 15:44b

For sure, we know that we shall be like him, or appear like him when we shall see him. For our citizenship is in heaven, from which also we look for the Saviour, the Lord Jesus Christ, 21who shall change our lowly body, that it may be fashioned like his glorious body, according to the working by which he is able even to subdue all things unto himself. Philippians 3:20-21

The scene of Rapture of the Saints will be similar to the scene that Jesus revealed to Peter, James and John on the mount of transfiguration. Let us consider the passage in Matthew 17:1-3;

And after six days, Jesus taketh Peter, James, and John, his brother, and bringeth them up into a high mountain privately, and was transfigured before them: and his face did shine as the sun, and his raiment— was as white as the light. And behold, there appeared unto them Moses and Elijah talking with him.

According to the New Scofield Study Bible; the transfiguration scene contains in miniature all the elements of the future Kingdom in manifestation:

- The Lord Jesus, not in humiliation but in glory.
- Moses, in glory, representative of the redeemed that have passed through death into the Kingdom.
- Elijah, in glory, representative of the redeemed that have entered the Kingdom by transformation.

Immediately after the transfiguration experience, the Lord Jesus warned the three disciples to keep this revelation secret until the Son of man is glorified. Even Apostle Paul, in his teachings to the Corinthians, called this a *mystery*. Today I call it a revelation.

The Anti-Christ

In the definition of rapture, I mentioned that this wonderful experience will take place before the destruction of the beast, the false prophet and those that shall receive the mark of the beast.

The beast here is the anti Christ who will be the leader of the next *world empire*. He shall make war with the saints. But finally, he shall be destroyed in the lake of fire.

A study of the book of Revelation Chapter 13 will reveal certain things about the beast and the false prophet.

And I stood upon the sand of the sea, and saw a <u>beast</u> rise up out of the <u>sea</u>, having seven heads and <u>ten horns</u>, and upon his horns ten crowns and upon his heads the name of blasphemy. Revelation 13:1 (underlining mine)

The Beast

The beast represents the Roman Empire which shall rise up again from fragments. This is Daniel's fourth beast (Daniel 7:7-8). It also represents the emperor of this empire. In other words, the beast represents the next world power within the region of Europe and the Middle East.

The Sea

The sea here represents the people, multitudes, nations and tongues.

And he saith unto me, the waters which thou sawest, where the whore sitteth, are peoples, and multitudes, and nations, and tongues. Revelation 17:15

The Ten Horns

The ten horns are explained in Daniel 7:24 and Revelation 17:12 to be ten kings. This shall be the last form of gentile world power; a confederation of ten or more nations which will be a revival of the old Roman Empire.

And the beast which I saw was like unto a leopard, and his feet like the feet of a bear, and his mouth like the mouth of a lion; and the <u>dragon</u> gave him his power, and his throne, and great authority. (underlining mine)Revelation 13:2

The beast was like a leopard, and had the feature like that of a bear and a lion. In Daniel 7:4-6, three animals were seen; a lion, a bear and a leopard. They are symbols of the empires that preceded the Romans Empire. Hence, the awakening of the Roman or European Empire will incorporate and even extend its boundaries beyond the old Babylon, Persia and Macedonia or Greek.

The Dragon

The dragon here is the Devil, that old serpent, who is Satan (Revelation 20:2).

The dragon gave him his power. Revelation 13:2c

The devil shall give all his power and authority to this last empire. Satan, through this empire, shall manipulate the nations with all his tricks to turn the hearts of the people from worshiping Almighty God.

And I saw one of his heads as though it was wounded to death; and his deadly wound was healed, and all the world wondered after the beast. Revelation 13:3

The temporal deadness of the Roman Empire and dismantling of some of its institutions, principles and policies is the meaning of the *deadly wound* on the head. The healing of the deadly wound shall be a restoration of a confederated empire of ten kingdoms and the world shall wonder at the emperor, the beast, over the wisdom of the confederated empire.

And they worshiped the dragon who gave power unto the beast; and they worshiped the beast, saying, who is like the beast? Who is able to make war with him? And there was given unto him a mouth speaking great things and blasphemies, and power was given unto him to continue forty and two months.

And he opened his mouth in blasphemy against God, to blaspheme his name and his tabernacle, and them that dwell in heaven. And it was given unto him to make war with the saints and to overcome them; and power was given him over all kindreds, and tongues and nations. And all that dwell upon the earth shall worship him, whose names are not written in the book of life of the Lamb slain from the foundation of the world. If any man has an ear, let him hear. He that leadeth into captivity shall go into captivity; he that killeth with the sword must be killed with the sword. Here is the patience and the faith of the saints. Revelation 13:4-10

These few verses above describe the characteristics and activities of this last beast, the Anti Christ. Therefore, let him who reads, understand the season; the coming together of the European countries, the manipulations and lordship of the British over the nations of the earth for centuries. And also of the queen that is arrayed in purple and scarlet colors that sits upon the affairs of many nations. (Revelation 17:1-13; Revelation 18:7)

The False Prophet

And I behold another beast coming out of the earth; and he had two horns like a lamb, and he spoke like a dragon. Revelation 13:11

The *another beast* is the false prophet that will work for the kingdom of the Anti Christ. There are many false prophets and antichrists; but this particular one, shall possess characteristics terrible and different from the previous ones and will arise after the awakening of the Roman or European Empire.

"*He had two horns like a lamb and he spoke like a dragon,*" means that the false prophet will be *a wolf in sheep clothing*. He shall be very religious and appear gentle and harmless while he carries the spirit of the devil to promote the government of the antichrist.

And he exerciseth all the power of the first beast before him and causeth the earth and them who dwell on it to worship the first beast, whose deadly wound was healed. And he doeth great wonders, so that he maketh fire come down from heaven on the earth in the sight of men. And deceiveth them that dwell on the earth by the means of those miracles which he had power to do in the sight of the beast, saying to them that dwell on the earth, that they should make an image of the beast, that had the wound by the sword and did live. Revelation 13:12-14

The false prophet will be a religious man with great political powers, (e.g a Pope or an Imam), and shall preach to promote the empire and the emperor, the beast.

And he had power to give life unto the image of the beast, that the image of the beast should both speak, and cause that as many as would not worship the image of the beast should be killed. And he causeth all, both small and great, rich and poor, free and enslaved, to receive a mark in their right hand, or in their foreheads. And that no man might buy or sell, except that he had the mark, or the name of the beast, or the number of his name. Here is wisdom. Let him that hath understanding count the number of the beast; for it is the number of a man; and his number is six hundred threescore and six. Revelation 13:15-18

The ability to give life to the image of the beast so that it could speak, shows the extent of the power of miracles that the false prophet shall possess. He will also possess political powers to put to death those that refuse to worship the image of the beast or support his 'religion'

Normal administrative services in the society and in government will require the acceptance of the religion of the false prophet and the worship of the beast. This compliance will be so strict that a *mark*, name or numbers will be used for personal identification. This is the number that is given in the Bible as '666'.

A law or decree to worship the beast or be identified with the false religion is not a strange concept to any Bible reader, religious student, or even a normal believer. In the days of Prophet Daniel, a similar law or decree was given twice.

In Daniel 3:4-5, when Shedrach, Meshach and Abednego were governors in the province of Babylon, it was decreed that everyone in Babylon and all the nations of the world should worship the golden image of king Nebuchadnezzar, or be thrown into a burning fiery furnace.

Again in Daniel 6:7-9, when Darius was the king of the Chaldeans, it was decreed that, everyone in the province of Mede Persia and every nation of the world should only pray to the royal status of king Darius or be cast into the dens of lions.

Therefore, in the last days, such laws and decrees that everyone must worship the beast and obtain a personal identity mark or be denied entry to schools, flights, or even the right to do business, will only be the repetition of what happened to the believers in Babylon and Persia. But God is able at all times, to defend and protect his children. As he did to the people of old, he will do it to his people in the last days.

Christians should therefore remember that whatever things were written in earlier times (Daniel's time), were written for our learning that we, through patience and comfort of the Scriptures, might have hope.

For whatsoever things were written aforetime were written for our learning, that we through patience and comfort of the Scriptures might have hope. Romans 15:4

Hence, such ungodly laws and decrees of those days were only pointing to what shall take place in the last days with the antichrist, the false prophet and the true believers of the Lord Jesus Christ. Wherefore, my brethren, these things are revealed that we might have hope and that we might be encouraged and know how to live in these last days. And that we might be like the three Hebrew boys who refused to bow to the threat of being thrown into the furnace of fire.

In the face of the threat, they declared with boldness; "O king Nebuchadnezar, O Mr. Antichrist or Rev. False Prophet, we are not careful to answer thee in this matter. If it be so, our God, whom we serve, is able to deliver us from the burning fiery furnace, and He will deliver us out of thine hands. But if not, be it known unto thee O king that we will not serve thy gods nor worship the golden image which thou hast set up, nor take the mark or the number of the beast." Daniel 3:16-18 (paraphrased)

Seeing then that we have a great high priest that is passed into the heavens, Jesus the Son of God, let us hold fast our profession. For we have not an high priest which cannot be touched with the feeling of our infirmities; but was in all points tempted like as we are, yet without sin. Let us therefore come boldly unto the throne of grace that we may obtain mercy, and find grace to help in time of need. Hebrews 4:14-16

From these explanations of the different terms involve in our definition of rapture, one can clearly recognise the importance of the rapture in the sequence of events that will take place in the Endtime. The deliverance of believers from the deadly trials and wraths of both the antichrist and the false prophet is one of the purposes of rapture. Let us turn now to the next chapter for details of this and other purposes of rapture.

CHAPTER TWO

The Purposes of Rapture

There are four major purposes or reasons why there will be a rapture.

Rapture is meant for the deliverance of believers from the wrath of God and from the deadly trials and persecutions of the antichrist.

Rapture is meant to transform the living believers of Jesus from earthly elements (mortal and corruptible) to become heavenly elements (immortal and incorruptible).

To bring the dead in Christ into the kingdom.

To reunite both the living and the dead in Christ in the kingdom.

Deliverance of Believers

The Lord has designed rapture to provide solution to believers against the dreadful and terrible day of the Lord. This is the day that judgment will be brought on the rebellious angels, the antichrist, the false prophets and all those that refuse to receive Jesus as their Lord and Saviour.

And I will show wonders in the heaven and in the earth: blood, and fire, and pillars of smoke. The sun shall be turned into darkness, and the moon into blood, <u>before the great and the terrible day of the Lord come</u>. And it shall come to pass that <u>whosoever shall call on the name of the Lord shall be delivered</u>; for in mount Zion and in Jerusalem shall be deliverance, as the Lord hath said, and in the remnant whom the Lord shall call. Joel 2:30-32 (Underlining mine)

The above Scripture is the prophecy of God through the Prophet, Joel. The plagues of blood, fire and smoke are the different tribulations that shall come upon the earth prior to the day of the Lord. Again, the sun shall be turned into darkness and the moon into blood and, of course, the powers of heaven shall be shaken.

These shall precede the signs of the second coming of the Son of God. These are the signs that will reveal in miniature the wrath of God upon the unbelievers. And after the dreadful signs shall the Son of God descend from heaven. The period of the antichrist will be terminated by the coming of Christ, and then shall come the great and terrible day of the Lord. Let us consider what Daniel wrote about this:

And he shall speak great words against the Most High, and shall wear out the saints of the Most High, and shall think to change the times and laws; and they shall be given into his hand until a time and times and the dividing of time. But the judgement shall sit and they shall take away his dominion, to consume and to destroy it unto the end,. Daniel 7:25 – 26

At the peak of the government of the antichrist while the world will be rejoicing against the saints, judgment shall sit in heaven and the Son of God shall come in His great power to terminate and to destroy forever the rule of the wicked.

In his teaching to the disciples about the signs of the Endtime, Jesus said;

"And immediately after the tribulations of those days shall the sun be darkened, and the moon shall not give its light, and the stars shall fall from heaven, and the powers of the heavens shall be shaken. And then shall appear the sign of the Son of man in heaven; and shall all the tribes of the earth mourn, and they shall see the Son of man coming in the clouds of heaven with power and great glory" Matthew 24:29 -30

Now, the teaching of Jesus in the above Scripture and the prophecy in Joel 2:30-32 are similar because they both point to the same event and the same period of time. They also reveal similar natural disasters before the "day of the Lord".

The tribulations of those days shall be administered by the wicked and dictatorial leader of the revived Roman Empire or European Union. And of course, God will give it into his hands to torment the earth and even the saints for a particular period of time. This period of time shall be explained in the next chapter, The Period of Rapture. When the sign of the Son of man appears in heaven, the operators of the wicked government of the antichrist and the false prophet shall grieve. The recipient of the identity and mark of the beast shall be caught unawares and they shall despair in regret of their unbelief.

But the day of the Lord will come like a thief in the night, in which the heaven will pass with the great noise, and the elements shall melt with fervent heat, the earth also, and the works that are in it, shall be burnt up. 2 Peter 3:10

The above Scripture clearly shows how extensive the destruction will be. It shall affect the earth in totality and the activities therein. The elements of the earth shall be melted with fervent heat - both the surface and under the surface of the earth will be affected. If this will actually take place, where will the saints be?

"The saints shall be raptured to meet the Lord in the air. Both the dead and the living in Christ shall be taken away from the earth to be with the Lord. Therefore the righteous will not be consumed together with the wicked. They shall not be subjected to the wraths of God against the wicked. We shall be redeemed from the earth to escape the fearful day of the Most High."

The Lord knoweth how to deliver the godly out of temptations, and to reserve the unjust unto the day of judgement to be punished. 2 Peter 2:9

The Wrath of God is for His Enemies;

God is jealous and the Lord revengeth; the Lord revengeth and is furious; the Lord will take vengeance on his adversaries, and he reserveth wrath for his enemies. Nahum 1:2

Again in Job 21:30, *That the wicked is reserved to the day of destruction? They shall be brought forth to the day of wrath.*

From the above Scriptures, we can see that God had prepared destruction for the unbelievers, the antichrist and the false prophets; while rapture had been prepared as a means of escape for the believers.

For God hath not appointed us to wrath but to obtain salvation by our Lord Jesus Christ 1Thessalonians 5:9

Hence, prior to the day of the wrath of God; two shall be in the field, one shall be taken in rapture and the other reserved for destruction. Two women shall be grinding at the mill, the one shall be taken, and the other left for destruction. We shall be separated before the destruction takes place.

The Transformation of the Living Believers

In chapter 1, I explained the transformation of the living believers in detail. From this explanation, we understand the need for and the importance of rapture before the saints can enter into the kingdom of heaven. At rapture, the living saints will be instantaneously and miraculously changed and they will find themselves possessing bodies entirely supernatural - the incorruptible swallowing up the corruptible.

Those Christians who are alive at the time of Christ's return, will share a universal experience as did Enoch and Elijah. We have not been told in details as to what the ultimate experience of these two men was, but one thing remains certain; those who never die will never need to be resurrected from the dead. Rapture, therefore, is purposed to be a means of possessing the heavenly body when the natural body has not passed through death.

Now this I say, brethren, that flesh and blood cannot inherit the kingdom of God; neither doth corruption inherit incorruption. For this corruptible must put on incorruption, and this mortal must put on immortality. So, when this corruptible shall have put on incorruption, and this mortal shall have put on immortality, then shall be brought to pass the saying that is written, Death is swallowed up in victory. O death, where is thy sting? O grave, where is thy victory? 1 Corinthians 15:50, 53-55

My brethren, it is only in rapture that we can overcome death because this mortal earthly body shall be changed into a heavenly body that need not die.

Bringing the Dead in Christ into the Kingdom

True believers of Christ are not damned in death, but they rest in sleep. To sleep is to rest from labour or from active service. Believers acquire eternal life at the acceptance of Jesus and they continue to live as long as they maintain their salvation by living in righteousness.

Therefore brethren, we are debtors, not to the flesh, to live after the flesh. For if ye live after the flesh ye shall die; but if ye through the spirit, do mortify the deeds of the body, ye shall live. Romans 8:12-13

For God sent Jesus Christ that whosoever shall believe in him should not perish but have everlasting life. Therefore, a believer, after a good work, can sleep or rest in death until the fulfillment of time. Paul once wrote to Timothy, saying, *"For I am now ready to be offered, and the time of my departure is at hand. I have fought a good fight, I have kept the faith. Henceforth, there is laid up for me a crown of righteousness which the Lord, the righteous judge shall give at that day and not to me only but unto all them also that love his appearing."* 2 Timothy 4:6-8.

Paul declared, "I am ready to sleep, rest from the battle which I know I have won." But, he continued, "I have to wait until the appearing of the Lord, so that I can obtain my crown". Hence, the period between Paul's death and the time that the Lord will appear is the period of Paul's rest.

Apart from Paul, there are other saints who have died in the Lord and some who were slain for the sake of the Gospel. They must all rest until the period of rapture whereby they will be called up for their reward from the Master.

And when he opened the fifth seal, I saw under the Alter the souls of them that were slain for the word of God, and for the testimony which they held. And they cried with a loud voice, saying, How long, O Lord, holy and true doest thou not judge and avenge our blood on them that dwell on the earth? And white robes were given unto every one of them; and it was said unto them that they should rest yet for a little season, until their fellow servants also and their brethren, that should be killed as they were, should be fulfilled. Revelation 6:9-11

And I heard a voice from heaven saying unto me, Write, Blessed are the dead who die in the Lord from henceforth. Yea, saith the Spirit, that they may rest from their labors and their works to follow them. Revelation 14:13

Rapture is therefore the means by which the dead or those that sleep in Christ will be received up into the kingdom.

But I would not have you to be ignorant, brethren, concerning them who are asleep, that ye sorrow not, even as others who have no hope. For the Lord himself shall descend from heaven with a shout, with the voice of the archangel, and with the trump of God; and the dead in Christ shall rise first. 1 Thessalonians 4:16

It is clear here that when a believer dies, he does not go into the kingdom immediately; nor does he receive the crown or his reward instantly. He or she must wait until the time of rapture, when the Lord himself will descend to receive the saints into the kingdom. Then, that believer will be resurrected and clothed to meet the Lord in the air, where the life of his reward will begin.

Blessed and holy is he that hath part in the first resurrection; on such the second death hath no power, but they shall be priests of God and of Christ and shall reign with him a thousand years. Revelation 20:6

The saints, after the rapture, will begin their life of reward and shall reign forever, even after the millennial rule as they continue with the Lord faithfully; for the second death shall not have power over them.

One may rightly ask; "where will the saints who are asleep in the Lord wait?" Let us consider what King Solomon wrote in his days:
Then shall the dust return to the earth as it was, and the spirit shall return unto God, who gaveth it. Ecclesiastes 12:7

And again, *For that which befalleth the sons of men befalleth the beasts. Even one thing befallleth them: as the one dieth, so dieth the other; Yea, they have all one breath, so that a man hath no pre-eminence above a beast; for all is vanity. All go unto one place; all are of the dust, and all turn to dust again. Who knoweth the spirit of a man that goeth upward, and the spirit of the beast that goeth downward to the earth?* Ecclesiastes 3:19-21

The teaching of King Solomon in these Scriptures is clear. At death, man's body returns to the dust, but the destiny of his spirit is upward, toward God. What takes place when the spirit of man at death is released from the body and is brought before God?

First, this appearance of the spirit of man before God is not the final Judgment, which will take place only after the resurrection of the dead.

Secondly, the spirit of the wicked and the ungodly man can have no permanent access to the presence of God. We may therefore conclude that the appearance of the spirit of man before God immediately after death is for one main purpose: to hear the divine sentence appointing to each spirit the state and the place it must occupy from the time of death to the time of resurrection and final judgment. Thereafter, each spirit is consigned to its duly appointed state and place and continues there until called forth again at the resurrection of the dead.

And when he had opened the fifth seal, I saw under the alter the soul of them that were slain for the word of God, and for the testimony which they held. And they cried with a loud voice, saying, How long, O Lord, holy and true, does thou not judge and avenge our blood on them that dwell on the earth? And white robes were given unto every one of them; and it was said unto them that they should rest for a little season, until their fellow servants also and their brethren, that should be killed as they were, should be fulfilled. Revelation 6:9-11

This Scripture shows that the spirits of the saints that died were not together with those of the sinners for the saints were under the Alter (the sanctuary of God). The spirits will continue to be in this state until the rapture.

Reuniting the Living and the Dead in the Kingdom

The temporal separation of believers and loved ones in Christ whenever death occurs, normally brings sorrow to the heart of the ones left behind. The death of an unbelieving friend, mother, father, or colleague is a real painful lost. This is because the fellowship they had, is forever terminated. A man who lives and dies without believing in Jesus Christ is condemned, and is totally separated from the redeemed of Christ.

For God so loved the world that He gave His only begotten son, that whosoever believeth in Him should not perish but have everlasting life. He that believeth on Him is not condemned; but he that believeth not is condemned already, because he hath not believed in the name of the only begotten son of God. John 3:16-18

While those that believed shall have everlasting life, those that believed not, shall be damned forever. After death, those that are redeemed cannot dwell or fellowship together with the condemned.

Therefore, the ungodly shall not stand in the judgement, nor sinners in the congregation of the righteous. For the Lord knoweth the way of the righteous; but the way of the ungodly shall perish. Psalm 1:5-6.

The ungodly or the sinners will not stand in judgment since they refused to believe in the son of God, Christ, the Saviour of the world. They will therefore, be separated from the congregation of the righteous - those that believed in Jesus and walked with Him. Hence, the two parties can never meet to fellowship either in death or during resurrection.

Let us consider the account of Lazarus and the rich man.

There was a certain rich man, which was clothed in purple and fine linen, and fared sumptuously every day: And there was a certain beggar named Lazarus, which was laid at his gate, full of sores, And desiring to be fed with the crumbs which fell from the rich man's table: moreover the dogs came and licked his sores. And it came to pass, that the beggar died, and was carried by the angels into Abraham's bosom: the rich man also died, and was buried; And in hell he lift up his eyes, being in torments, and seeth Abraham afar off, and Lazarus in his bosom. And he cried and said, Father Abraham, have mercy on me, and send Lazarus, that he may dip the tip of his finger in water, and cool my tongue; for I am tormented in this flame. But Abraham said, Son, remember that thou in thy lifetime receivedst thy good things, and likewise Lazarus evil things: but now he is comforted, and thou art tormented. And beside all this, between us and you there is a great gulf fixed: so that they which would pass from hence to you cannot; neither can they pass to us, that would come from thence. Luke 16: 19-26

This is a well known portion of the Scripture narrated by Christ himself while on earth. Lazarus, although poor, loved the Lord and the rich man who had all at his will, lived without faith in God. After death, both Lazarus and the rich man found themselves within the realm of the departed spirits called Sheol in Hebrew and Hades in Greek but their destinies there were quite different.

The rich man's spirit was in a place of torment; the spirit of Lazarus was in a place of rest. Between these two places was fixed an impassable gulf that could not be crossed from either side even by the spirits. The place of rest, set apart for the departed spirits of the righteous, here is called, Abraham's bosom. This title indicates that this place is ordained for the spirit of all those who, in their earthly pilgrimage, followed in the footsteps of faith and obedience marked out by Abraham, who for this reason, is called the father of all those who believe.

Apart from the *rich man* episode in the Bible, there were men who lived *Christless* lives and died. Before their death, they testified of their impending doom to perdition and total separation.

On the other hand, we can imagine the joy that believers of Jesus Christ experience when they are called to rest from their labour. This joy is overwhelming, and the state of abode of the believers is the opposite to that of the unbelievers.

Augustus M. Toplady, was the writer of the song, 'Rock of ages, cleft for me, Let me hid myself in thee.' Leaping out of the world to the great beyond, he said, "O what delights! Who can fathom the joy of the third heaven? All is light, light, light - the brightness of His glory. O come, Lord Jesus, come quickly." [1]

Like many of us, Daniel was bothered about what shall become of him and his people concerning the interpretation of the dream of King Nebuchadnezzar (in Daniel chapter 2) and the prophecies of the Endtime. He was bothered whether he would live to witness all the prophecies being fulfilled, but God told him that he would rest in death until rapture.

But go thou thy way till the end be; for thou shall rest, and stand in thy lot at the end of the days. Daniel 12:13.

At rapture therefore, the dead in Christ will rise first. They shall be gathered from Abraham's bosom (Luke 16:22). They shall be called up from under the altar (Revelation 6:9). They shall be raised incorruptible and be made ready in the cloud. Then we, who are alive and remain, shall be caught up with them in the cloud. And together, both those who are raised from death and those that are changed from the natural body, shall meet the Lord in the air. Hallelujah!

Now, consider this carefully:

[13]But I will not have you ignorant, brethren, concerning them who are asleep, that ye sorrow not, even as others who have no hope. [14]For if we believe that Jesus died and rose again, even so them also who sleep in Jesus will God bring with him. [15]For this we say unto you by the word of the Lord, that we who are alive and remain unto the coming of the Lord shall not precede them who are asleep.
[16]For the Lord himself shall descend from heaven with a shout, with the voice of the archangel, with the trump of God; and the dead in Christ shall rise first; [17]then we which are alive and remain shall be caught up together with them in the clouds, to meet the Lord in the air; and so shall we ever be

with the Lord. ^{18}Wherefore comfort one another with these words. 1 Thessalonians 4:13-18.

The above Scripture reveals that there will be a reunification, a coming together of the dead and the living in one fold. There will be a re-fellowship of those that departed in death and those that buried them in sorrows. And together, we shall meet with the Lord Jesus as a congregation of believers. This is one of the benefits of rapture.

---

[1] This information is extracted from the Christian tract - Heaven or Hell from the DCLM)

CHAPTER 3

The Period of Rapture

The period of rapture, an ignored truth, is fully recorded in the Scriptures. It is the major aim of the book of Daniel. It is also the purpose of the book of Revelation, where detailed explanations are given. In fact, the book of Revelation is the detailed explanation of the mysteries of the book of Daniel. Hence, the period of rapture is a fascinating revelation, though the context may be contrary to the accepted knowledge of many Christians, yet this truth cannot be ignored.

Let me start with a leading statement before the explanations and supporting Scriptures.

All believers, including those of the Jewish and the Gentile nations will be raptured at the second coming of the Lord Jesus after the great tribulations, and before the destruction of the antichrist (the beast), his false prophet and the unbelievers.

This statement contain the period of four different events that will mark the End of Age;

1. The Great Tribulations
2. The Second Coming of Christ
3. The Rapture
4. The Destruction

It is one thing to have knowledge of the events; it is another thing to know the order in which the events have been programmed in the Bible. It is not enough to have ideas about the truth but we need freedom and boldness to know the truth. It is only when one knows the truth that freedom is obtained. (John 8:32)

According to the teaching or lecture titled, "Signs of the End of Age" given by Jesus Christ to the disciples in Matthew 24:3-35; the period of the events of the Endtime and of the End of Age can be arranged in the descending order as follows:

Beginning of Sorrows (Matthew 24:5-8)
- Wars, nations against nations, famines, pestilences, earthquakes.

Great Tribulation (Matthew 24:9-24)
- The opening of the 4th seal, the rise of the antichrist to afflict the saints, the opening of the 5th, 6th and the 7th seals.
(Revelation 6:1-17; Revelation chapters 8, 9, 10, 11)

The Second Coming of Christ
(Matthew 24:26-30)

The Rapture of the Saints
(Matthew 24:31)

The Destruction
(Revelation 16:1-2)
- The destruction of the beast (antichrist), false prophet, the unbelievers and the recipients of the mark of the antichrist.
(Rev. 15:1; Rev. 16: 3-21; Rev. 19:17-21; Rev. 20:1-3)

The Millennial Reign of the Saints with Christ
(Revelation 20:4)

The Release of Satan for a Limited Time
(Revelation 20:7-10)

The White Throne Judgment
(Revelation 20:11-15)

New life in Paradise, new Heaven and new Earth
(Revelation 21:1-6)

Through the special grace of God and the revelation from the Holy Spirit, the sequence of events illustrated above is based on the Scriptures. As we all know, the particular time (year, day, hour or second) for these events are nowhere mentioned in the Bible but the beginning of the first will only lead to the second since God is not an author of confusion. If it has pleased Him to set the order then He will also execute them accordingly even if we doubt it.

The time duration of one event would certainly not be the same for the next event. Although the duration is given for some events like the rule of the antichrist and the millennial rule of Christ, there is need for patience and genuineness of heart.

Since this book is centered on rapture, I shall dwell with the detail descriptions of the events between "the Period of the Beginning of Sorrows" and "the Period of Destruction of Unbelievers." Hence, I will start with the period of "The Beginning of Sorrows". Although I may not go into all details of some in-depth revelations, but all necessary information shall be given.

1. The Beginning of Sorrows

Let us first consider the text from Matthew 24:3-8

And as He sat upon the Mount of Olives, the disciples came unto Him privately, saying, tell us, when shall be the sign of thy coming, and of the end the age.

The disciples of Jesus might have been troubled every time their master spoke about the coming of the kingdom of God. And like us, they were eager to know the timing of the coming kingdom, the second coming of Christ and the restoration of the kingdom to Israel. They were also anxious to know of the signs of the end of age. There are many Christian today who are only interested in the elementary teaching of Christianity: Salvation, Baptism, Laying on of hands, Speaking in tongues and Holiness. But the deeper knowledge of the things of God gets them confused. Paul called these Christians "babies" who have need of milk (Hebrews 5:11-14). Most people normally refer to new converts or ordinary members of the church as such babies.

Controversially the writer of Hebrews was referring to the pastors, teachers, evangelists and spirit-filled believers who are satisfied with their knowledge of the elementary doctrines of the Bible; who remained convicted with the truth they obtained in the Seminary, Bible colleges and from great spiritual fathers. Such people consider themselves to know it all and so it becomes difficult for them to seek for deeper revelations in God's Word.

These are unlike Prophet Daniel who was interested to know the certainty of the dream and the details of every revelation. (Daniel 7:15-16, Daniel 9:22, 10:14, 12:8)

These are also unlike the twelve disciples of Jesus, who were interested to understand the meaning of every parable and of course, the detail of the signs of the second coming of Christ and of the End of Age. (Matthew 13:36; 17:19; 24:3)

Returning to our text in Matthew 24:3, the disciples requested Jesus to tell them of the time of his second coming. Consider the question:
Tell us when shall these things be?
And what shall be the sign......?

And Jesus did not consider this question to be irreverent or offensive as others may consider today. He patiently began to teach them or lecture them on the events of the Endtime starting with the period of light affliction, tagged "the Beginning of Sorrows".

And ye shall hear of wars and rumors of wars; see that ye be not troubled; for all these things must come to pass, but the end is not yet. For nation shall rise against nation, and kingdom against kingdom; and there shall be famines, and pestilences, and earthquakes, in various places. All these are the beginning of sorrows. Matthew 24:6-8

The happenings or the things that shall take place in this period are clearly stated in the above Scripture. These include:
- Wars - like the 1ˢᵗ and 2ⁿᵈ World Wars and civil wars in many nations of the world.
- Rumors of wars - Like the continuous threat by North Korea, Hamas, Iran and Hezbollah against USA, Israel and other nations.
- Nation against nation.
- Famines -- Like in Russia, Rwanda and Somalia in the nineties.

Pestilences -Like AIDS, Mad Cow Disease (BSE), EBOLA, COVID-19.
- Earthquakes - Like those in Turkey, Greece, Haiti, and Japan in the nineties.

The world has experienced the above mentioned troubles over and over, yet the end has not come. Jesus said, *"this period is the beginning of sorrows."* The beginning of the troubles that will continue. The manifestation of these troubles, wars, pestilence, and earthquakes is the confirmation that the other promises will be fulfilled.

In Matthew 24:6b we read: but the end is not yet. These are just the signs of the beginning. Christians should consider the words that Jesus spoke to be truthful. We have gone through the time of the "Beginning of Sorrows".

2. The Great Tribulation

The period of the great tribulation is marked with the opening of the 4th seal in Revelation 6:7-8.

And when he had opened the fourth seal, I heard the voice of the fourth living creature say come. And I looked and behold, a pale horse, and his name that sat on him was Death, and Hades followed with him. And power was given to them over the fourth part of the earth to kill with sword, and with hunger, and with death, and with the beasts of the earth.
The opening of the 4th seal reveals a horse carrying Death and Hades. Death is the result of sin.

For the wages of sin is death. Roman 6:23

Hades is Hell. This is the period that most people will be received down in hell. Because iniquity shall abound, the love of many shall grow cold. Many shall give up their salvation and so Hades shall receive many that Death shall slay.

The killing shall be with Swords, Hunger, Death, and with the Beasts of the earth. The killing with swords shall be the wars and violence. Killings with hunger shall be as the result of lack of food, bad policies, high cost and of course adverse effect of wars. Killings with death shall be the rampant passing away of both young and old through one reason or the other e.g sickness, virus outbreaks, terror attacks, accidents with different medium, spirit of murdering and so on. Killing with the beast of the earth will be the manifestation of the antichrist and the false prophet (Ezekiel 14:21). Who shall make war even with the saints and overcome them and shall kill many mercilessly.

And after this I saw in the night visions, and, behold, a fourth beast dreadful and terrible, and strong exceedingly, and it had great iron teeth; it devoured and broke in pieces, and stamped the residue with its feet; and it was diverse from all the beasts that was before it, and it had ten horns. I beheld, and the same horn made war with the saint, and prevailed against them. Daniel 7:7, 21

The fourth beast here is the Roman Empire. The Horn is the emperor. In chapter one of this book I explained the rise of the Roman empire from fragments after the temporary period of deadness which gives meaning to the deadly wound on the head as stated in Revelation 13:3.

In addition to this explanation in chapter one, let me add few things about the beast for better understanding of this period in which we are living today.

Thou, O king, sawest, and behold a great image. This great image, whose brightness was excellent, stood before thee; and the form thereof was terrible. This image's head was of fine gold, his breast and his arms of silver, his belly and his thighs of brass, his legs of iron, his feet part of iron and part of clay. Thou sawest till that a stone was cut out without hands, which smote the image upon his feet that were of iron and clay, and break them to pieces. Then was the iron, the clay, the brass, the silver, and the gold, broken to pieces together, and became like the chaff of the summer threshing floors; and the wind carried them away, that no place was found for them: and the stone that smote the image became a great mountain, and filled the whole earth. Daniel 2:31-35

This was the dream that the king of Babylon, king Nebuchadnezzar had. None of the wise men in Babylon except Daniel could understand this dream. The dream was the revelation of what shall take place in God's calendar from the period of king Nebuchadnezzar until the time of the end concerning the rule of the gentile or the government of the nations.

God placed Daniel in the kingdom of Babylon, gave the dream to the king who did not worship the true God so that the dream will receive enough publicity and attention. The revelation of the things of future is important to God so that his people will understand and have hope.

Let us now consider the meaning of this great image in the king's dream.

This is the dream; and we will tell the interpretation thereof before the king. Thou, O king, art a king of kings: for the God of heaven hath given thee a kingdom, power, and strength, and glory. And wheresoever the children of men dwell, the beasts of the field and the fowls of the heaven hath he given into thine hand, and hath made thee ruler over them all. Thou art this head of gold. And after thee shall arise another kingdom inferior to thee, and another third kingdom of brass, which shall bear rule over all the earth. And the fourth kingdom shall be strong as iron: forasmuch as iron breaketh in pieces and subdueth all things: and as iron that breaketh all these, shall it break in pieces and bruise. And whereas thou sawest the feet and toes, part of potters' clay, and part of iron, the kingdom shall be divided; but there shall be in it of the strength of the iron, forasmuch as thou sawest the iron mixed with miry clay. Daniel 2:36-41

The interpretation of the dream reveals the great image to represent the body of government of the nations starting with the Babylonian Empire as the head of gold.

In verse 37 and 38, King Nebuchadnezzar was divinely empowered over all the people and all the beast of the earth. He represents the head of gold in this dream (Daniel 2:32). He also represents the first beast which was like a lion and had eagle's wings in Daniel 7:4.

Following the Babylonian Empire was to be another world empire known as the Medo Persia. This is the silver part of the breast and arms of the image in Nebuchadnezzar's dream. (Daniel 2:32) This empire was also shown to Daniel in the form of a beast with appearance like a bear in Daniel 7:5.

The third world empire, the Greece Empire, is the belly of bronze of the image in the dream. It was also represented by the third beast with the appearance like the leopard in Daniel 7:6.

After the Greek Empire was to come another world empire and this we know was the Roman Empire which is represented by the "legs of iron" and "feet of iron and clay" in Nebuchadnezzar's dream. In Daniel 7:7, it is represented by the fourth beast, dreadful and terrible and diverse from all the beasts that were before it.

We have witnessed or heard of the Babylonian Empire, the Medo Persia Empire, the Greece Empire and also the Roman Empire. These are actually the fulfillment of the dreams and visions that king Nebuchadnezzar and Prophet Daniel had.

The last beast is important to every Christian now living because all the prophecies concerning this beast have not yet been fulfilled, since the antichrist will be one of the emperors of this empire.

The period in which we now live is the time of the revival of the Roman Empire which is coming stronger in the form of European Union.

And I saw one of his head as though it was wounded to death, and his deadly wound was healed. And the entire world wondered after the beast. Revelation 13:3

The healing of the deadly wound of one of the head of the beast will be the reformation of the former Roman Empire which is now represented by the European Union.

After this I saw in the night visions, and, behold, a fourth beast, dreadful and terrible and strong exceedingly, and it had great iron teeth; it devoured and brook in pieces, and stamped the residue with its feet; and it was diverse from all the beast that were before it, and it had ten horns. I considered the horns, and behold, there came up among them another little horn, before which there were three of the first horns plucked up by the roots; and, behold, in this horn were eyes like the eyes of man, and a mouth speaking great things. Daniel 7:7-8

The above are two long verses that give us the description and the character of the fourth beast which represents the Roman Empire. The complete interpretation of the terms used in the above verses are given below

And the ten horns out of this kingdom are ten kings that shall arise; and another shall rise after them, and he shall be diverse from the first, and he shall subdue three kings. And he shall speak great words against the Most High, and shall wear out the saints of the Most High, and think to change the times and the laws; and they shall be given into his hand until a time and times and the dividing of time. Daniel 7:24-25

When the European Union begins to operate one central government, there shall arise a leader that will be adorable in wisdom but terrible in his intentions. He shall stand against God's people and hate the name of Jesus Christ. This shall be the little horn and he shall make war with the Saint and shall kill many.
Read that again; he shall make war with the saints of the most high; not unserious Christian that could not make rapture as many may think. But saints filled with the Holy Spirit and speaking in tongues, Sanctified and

Justified by strong faith in the Lord Jesus. These are the people that can stand against the wiles of the antichrist although he shall kill many. He shall kill both believers and unbelievers because it shall be given into his hand to accomplish that. He shall change the laws and make it compulsory for people to be identified with the mark of the beast. But this period shall last for only forty-two months according to the prophecy in Revelation 11:1-2.

And there was given me a reed like a rod; and the angel stood saying Rise, and measure the temple of God, and the alter, and them that worship in it. But the court, which is outside the temple, leave out, and measure it not; for it is given unto the nations, and the holy city shall they tread under foot forty and two months.

The total period of the tribulation under the government of the antichrist shall be seven years, the one week of Daniel 9:27. This seven year period is divided, in the prophetic writings, into two equal halves of three and a half years each. The length of the periods is also referred to as *a time, and times, and half a time* (Rev. 12:14, Daniel 7:25; Daniel12:7); *forty and two months* (Rev. 11:2; 13:5); and 1260 days. (Rev. 11:3; 12:6) The second half of this seven-year period will be characterised by increasing cruelty on the part of the world ruler, and as a consequence, greater intensity of persecution and suffering.

Although the period of time of the great tribulation is specifically given as 42 months or 1260 days, but no one knows the actual day that Jesus shall return to take the saints away. Hence, knowledge and patience will take us through. This is the reason that Daniel wrote in Daniel 12:11-12 saying;

And from the time that the daily sacrifice shall be taken away, and the abomination that maketh desolate set up, there shall be a thousand two hundred and ninety days (1290 days). Blessed is he that waiteth, and cometh to the thousand three hundred five and thirty days (1335 days).

Although the period of the great tribulation is given as 42 months, 1260 days, or 1290 days, Daniel wrote and said, blessed is he that will wait even a little bit longer until 1335 days. Just like the parable of the ten virgins who took their lamps and went forth to meet the bridegroom in Matthew 25:1-13. Jesus told this parable to the disciple immediately after he had told them of the period of his second coming so that they will learn to exercise patience even in those days. God is never late but he had set time for everything.

Now, let us consider this parable of the ten virgins:

Then shall the kingdom of God be likened unto ten virgins, who took their lamps and went to meet the bridegroom. And five of them were wise, and five were foolish. They that were foolish took their lamps, and took no oil with them; but the wise took oil in their vessels with their lamps. While the bridegroom tarried they all slumbered and slept. And at midnight there was a cry made, behold, the bridegroom cometh; go ye out to meet him. Then all those virgins arose and trimmed their lamps. And the foolish said unto the wise, give us of your oil; for our lamps are gone out. But the wise answered, saying, not so else there be not enough for us and you; but go rather to them that sell, and buy for yourselves. And while they went to buy, the bridegroom came, and they that were ready went in with him to the marriage; and the door was shut. Afterward came also the other virgins, saying, Lord, Lord, open to us. But he answered and said; verily I say unto you, I know you not. Watch, therefore; for ye know neither the day nor the hour in which the Son of man cometh. Matthew 25:1-13

From the parable of the ten virgins, we can understand that the period and the day of the marriage were set; but the time, i.e. the hour and the minutes for the arrival of the bridegroom were not set. Because of this, the wise virgins carried extra oil in their lamps incase the arrival of the bridegroom is delayed. The foolish virgins thought that as long as the period was set and the day has come, the bridegroom would certainly arrive earlier; and so they were not prepared for any delay, hence, they carried no extra oil with them. The virgins who carried extra oil with them were called the wise virgins because they were prepared for patience in case of any delay. This is why Jesus conclusively warned in verse 13 of Matthew 25 saying;

Watch, therefore; for ye know neither the day nor the hour in which the Son of man cometh.

Although we are told of the period of the second coming of Christ, we are not told of the day and the hour. Therefore, we have to be watchful. Daniel also said, as we read earlier, that the period of tribulation will last for only three and a half years or 1290 days after which Christ will come. He also warned and said, "blessed is the one that will be prepared to wait a little longer up to 1335 days."

An important operator in this evil government will be the false prophet who will deceive many with false miracles (Rev. 13:11 – 18)

And because of the hard times and the search for miracles, many shall be forced to worship the beast. Christians who shall refuse to accept this evil shall be afflicted and some killed. *And except those days were shortened, no flesh could survive it; but for the elect's sake those days shall be shortened.* Matthew 24:22.

When the Bible talks of the elects, it refers to those whose names are in the Book of Life both of the Israelites and of the Gentiles Saints according to the Gospel in the books of Ephesians and Galatians.

Blessed be the God and Father of our Lord Jesus Christ, who had bless us with all spiritual blessings in heavenly places in Christ, according as he hath chosen (elected) us in him before the foundation of the world, that we should be holy and without blame before him, in love. Having predestinated us unto the adoption of sons by Christ Jesus to himself, according to the good pleasure of his will, to the praise of the glory of his grace, wherein he hath made us accepted in the beloved. Ephesians 1:3-5

And also in Galatians 3:26-29;

For ye are all the sons of God by faith in Christ Jesus, for as many of us as have been baptized into Christ have put on Christ. There is neither Jew nor Greek, there is neither bond nor free, there is neither male nor female; for ye are all one in Christ Jesus. And if ye be Christ's, then are ye Abraham's Seed and heirs according to promise.

Let us also consider what Apostle Peter wrote to the saints in Asia who were Jews by birth:

Peter, an apostle of Jesus Christ, to the sojourners scattered throughout Pontus, Galatia Cappadocia, Asia and Bithynia, Elect according to the fore knowledge of God, the Father, through sanctification of the Spirit, unto obedience and sprinkling of the blood of Jesus Christ: Grace unto you, and peace, be multiplied. 1 Peter 1:2

The above three portions of the Scriptures states clearly that all Christians are the elected or chosen of God and are all Abraham's seed and heirs to God's kingdom. When Apostle Paul was writing to the saints in Ephesus and Galatia; he addressed them and acknowledged them as the "Elects of God." In the same way, when Apostle Peter was writing to the Jews that were in Asia, he also addressed them and called them the "Elects of God." Therefore, there is neither Jew nor Greek in Christ Jesus, for we are all Elects of God in Christ. Hence all Elects that shall be alive in the days of the antichrist shall all pass through the Great Tribulations before the rapture takes place.

The dogma and teaching that the saints of the gentile nations will be raptured before the Great Tribulation have no base proof within the Scriptures. This is what we have been made to believe by the Catholic doctrine, and we still believe in this because of the terrors of the Great Tribulation. It is time we search the Scriptures, and begin to believe the truth, whether it conforms to the doctrines of our local churches or not. There are many Christians who are Jews by birth and who are fully committed to God as are Christians from the gentile nations. Some people believe that the good Christians from the gentile nations will be raptured before the Great Tribulations while those of the Jewish nation (God's own people) will be made to pass through the Great Tribulations before they are raptured. This is wrong. There is no second rapture in the Bible.

After the period of the Great Tribulation, comes the period of our great expectation - The Second coming of Christ.

3. The Second Coming of Jesus Christ

The Second Coming of Christ is the event that will bring to absolute end the terrible rule of the antichrist and of the false prophet.

Thou sawest until a stone was cut out without hands, which smote the image upon its feet that were of iron and clay and broke them into pieces. Daniel 2:34

This image with its different parts, as we have already seen, is the gentile rule and the different empires. The feet of iron and clay represent, of course, the Roman Empire. The stone that was cut without hands is the Second Coming of Christ that will take place during the last empire namely the revived Roman Empire or the European Union.

And in the days of these kings shall the God of heaven set up a kingdom, which shall never be destroyed; and the kingdom shall not be left to other people, but it shall break in pieces and consume all these kingdoms and it shall stands forever.

For as much as thou sawest that the stone was cut out of the mountain without hands, and it broke in pieces the iron, the bronze, the clay, the silver and the gold, the great God hath made known to the king what shall come to pass hereafter; and the dream is certain, and the interpretation of it is sure. Daniel 2:44-45

The God of heaven showed to Nebuchadnezzar that he will take over the kingdom of the earth from man during the last empire. The stone that was cut out without hands is the Second Coming of Christ, and he is coming to set the kingdom of heaven on earth forever.
Immediately after the tribulation of those days shall the sun be darkened and the moon shall not give its light, and the stars shall fall from heaven, and the powers of the heavens shall be shaken. And then shall appear the sign of the Son of man in heaven; and then shall all the tribes of the earth mourn, and they shall see the Son of man coming in the clouds of heaven with power and great glory. Matthew 24:29-30

The Second Coming of Christ will be after the Great Tribulation. Christians who will be alive in those days shall be afflicted, but they need to continue to trust and believe the promises of Christ about his coming even in the midst of severe trials and tribulations.

Let not your heart be troubled, ye believe in God, believe also in Me. And if I go and prepare a place for you, I will come again and receive you unto myself, that where I am, there ye may be also. John 14: 1, 3

Before the period of His coming, there will be great tribulations, but Jesus said, "Let not your heart be troubled." In other words, do not doubt my coming or promises, like John who sent the disciples to confirm whether Jesus was the Christ because of the great trials that he (John) went through.

History proves that Jesus once lived and walked the streets of this world. That He was crucified and buried; and that He arose from the dead and went to heaven: promising to return. So He will surely come again. Many believers might ask, "But when will He come?" The answer is clearly given by the Lord himself when the disciples asked Him of the signs of His second coming. Let's consider his answer in Matthew 24:15

When ye, therefore, shall see the abomination of desolation spoken of by Daniel the Prophet, stand in the holy place (whosoever readeth let him understand).

The above verse marks the beginning of the Great Tribulation. After wars, famine, earthquakes and other plagues; the manifestation of the beast to fight and take over Jerusalem will be one of the signs of the Second Coming of Jesus Christ. Verse 16 of the same chapter reads;

Then let them who are in Judea flee into the mountains.

The word 'flee ' here simply means 'depart in haste'. So, when the antichrist takes over the government of Jerusalem, let the Christians depart in haste from the city to avoid unnecessary torture and killing. This shall be similar to what Joseph and Mary did when they departed from Bethlehem to avoid Jesus, their son, being killed by King Herod.

For then shall be great tribulation, such as was not since the beginning of the world to this time, no, nor ever shall be. And except those days should be shortened, there should no flesh be saved; but for the elect's sake, those days shall be shortened. Matthew 24:21-22

Clearly, the Scripture is saying that the worst tribulation will take place immediately once the government of the antichrist takes over Jerusalem. The tribulation will be so terrible that even the elects (God's chosen people, both Jew and gentile whose names are in the Book of Life), will narrowly survive it. At the peak of this government of the antichrist, the Son of God will come in the Power of His great glory.

Immediately after the tribulation of those days shall the sun be darkened then shall appear the sign of the Son of man in heaven; and then shall all the tribes of the earth mourn, and they shall see the Son of man coming in the clouds of heaven with power and great glory. Matthew 24:29-30

When the period of Great Tribulation, which shall last for forty two months, beginning from the time that the holy place in Jerusalem is overtaken by other nations, is completed, the Lord will return to take the saints away in rapture. There shall be no coup de tat and no handing over to another emperor or empire, for it will be a sudden occurrence. Referring back to the book of Daniel concerning this, we read in Daniel 7:25-27;

And he shall speak great words against the Most High, and shall wear out the saints of the Most High; and think to change the time and the laws and they shall be given into his hands until a time and times and the dividing of time. But the judgement shall sit; and they shall take away his dominion, to consume and to destroy it unto the end. And the kingdom and dominion, and the greatness of the kingdom under the whole heaven, shall be given to the people of the saints of the Most High, whose kingdom is an everlasting kingdom, and all dominions shall serve and obey him.

While the wicked ruler, the antichrist, shall continuously blaspheme the name of God, and afflict the saints with anti human laws, his heart will become so proud in anticipation that he is all powerful; the Bible says,

"Judgment shall sit to take away, consume and destroy his dominion unto the end". In other words, Christ shall appear suddenly; and power shall change hands and Christians will take over dominion of government of the whole earth. Brethren, this is the period when Christ will come; but the particular DAY (DATE) and the HOUR (TIME) is known unto the Father only.

4. The Period of Rapture of the Saints

This is the period that most people are really confused about. Some teachers and Bible scholars believe, and also teach, that the period of Rapture will come before the period of the Great Tribulation and the Second Coming of Christ. However, as we have earlier read in this chapter, the Scripture does not support this believe and so there is need for a change of mind. There are two important reasons why we must change our minds on this issue. And these are;

When the Great Tribulation actually comes, while the believers have not yet been raptured, those who believed otherwise will be frustrated and may think that rapture is not real. They may even lose the hope of their salvation and decide to join the antichrist and accept the mark of the beast.

When we know the truth that the Great Tribulation will actually come before the Rapture of the Saints or the Second Coming of Christ, then we shall be bold even in the days of the antichrist to do exploits for our God.

First, let us consider our text in Matthew Chapter 24. The use of the words like *"When", "Immediately After"* and *"And Then"* in verses 15, 21, 29 and 30; shows that the sequence of events of the end shall be sequential and not random. The period of Rapture of the Saints is therefore recorded to take place after the Great Tribulation and when the Lord shall appear in the cloud with His angles.

When ye therefore shall see the abomination of desolation, spoken of by Daniel the prophet, stand in the holy place, (whosoever readeth let him understand) for then shall be great tribulation, Such as was not since the beginning of the world... Immediately after the tribulation of those days, shall the sun be darkened... And then shall appear the sign of the Son of man in heaven...And he shall send his angels with a great sound of a trumpet, and they shall gather together his elect from the four winds, from one end of heaven to the other. Matthew 24:29-31

It is clearly stated here that there will be great tribulation: and immediately after that, Jesus will come, and then, the rapture will follow. This is the sequence according to the account given by Christ himself in this Scripture. And this is what we are supposed to believe and teach instead of the human-formulated theories.

Again, the saints will be gathered at the sound of the last trumpet. Let us also consider what this means. Paul, in one of his letters, treats the rapture as a mystery because his audience could not absorb the full revelation then.

Behold, I show you a <u>mystery:</u> we shall not all sleep but we shall be changed, In a moment, in the twinkling of an eye, at the last trump; for the trumpet shall sound, and the dead shall be raised incorruptible, and we shall be changed. 1 Corinthians 15:51-52 (Underlining mine)

What Paul called a mystery has become a revelation in this book. The gathering of the saints, both the dead and the living at the sound of the (last) trumpet is found at least in four portions of the Scriptures: 1 Corinthians 15:52, 1 Thessalonians 4:16, Mathew 24:31 and Revelation 11:15.

In the book of Revelation, chapter 6 and 7, the seals of the Endetime manifestations are opened. In the seventh seal are the seven trumpets (Revelation 8:1-2). And, at the sound of the last trumpet, the rapture will take place.

And the seven Angel sounded; and there were great voices in heaven, saying the kingdom of this world is become the kingdom of our Lord, and his Christ and he shall reign forever and ever. And the four and the twenty Elders, who sat before God on their thrones, fell upon their faces and worshiped God, Saying, We give thee thanks, O Lord God Almighty, who art, and was, and art to come, because thou hast taken to thee thy great power, and hast reigned. And the nations were angry, and thy wrath is come, and the time of the dead, that they should be judged, and that thou shouldest give reward unto thy servants, the prophets, and to the saints, and them that fear thy name, small and great, and shouldest destroy them who destroy the earth. Revelation 11:15-18

The sound of the trumpet in this Scripture is the same as in 1 Corinthians 15:52, 1Thessalonians 4:16, and Matthew 24:31. This is the sound of the trumpet that will go forth before the rapture and it contains nothing else but the fulfilment of the prophecy of the Second Coming of our Lord and the Rapture of His Saints. Let us also compare Revelation 11:18, as recorded above, with Matthew 24:30

And then shall appear the sign of the Son of man in heaven: and then shall all the tribes of the earth mourn, and they shall see the Son of man coming in the clouds of heaven with power and great glory.

In both Scriptures, the nations shall be angered at the appearing of the Lord because they shall see the Son of man coming to take over the government of this world. At this time, the dead that were told to wait a while in Revelation 6:11 will be judged.

The crown and the reward that Paul awaits after a good fight of faith in 2 Timothy 4:7-8 will be given to God's servants, prophets, saints and all those that fear the name of the Lord. In simple terms, the Rapture of the Saints will take place. This was written for our understanding that we might know what shall befall the world in the last days. This was also written that we might not be confused with the unscriptural ideas of some people, which portray our fears rather than the truth about the Great Tribulation. It was to guard against ideas like these that Apostle Paul wrote to the saints in Thessalonica, saying;

Now we beseech you brethren, <u>by the coming of our Lord Jesus Christ, and by our gathering together unto him</u> (which is the rapture of the saints), that ye be not soon shaken in mind, or be troubled, neither by spirit, nor by word nor by letter as from us, as that the day of the Lord is present. <u>Let no</u>

man deceive you by any means; for that day shall not come, except there come the falling away first, and that man of sin be revealed, the son of perdition, Who opposeth and exalted himself above all that is called God, or that is worshiped, so that He as God, sitteth in the temple of God, showing himself that he is God. 2 Thessalonians 2:1-4 (Underlining mine)

Now, brethren please read the underlined sentences again but this time with more attention: by the coming of our Lord Jesus Christ, and by our gathering unto him; Let no man deceive you by any means; for that day shall not come, except there come the falling away first, and that man of sin be revealed, the son of perdition.

God has set the sequence that is recorded in this Scripture, and so He cannot do it any other way, because, He is not the author of confusion. The coming of the Lord and the gathering unto him is simply the Second Coming of Jesus Christ and the Rapture of the Saints. Concerning this, Apostle Paul wrote to the people of Thessalonica, (not the Jews or the Israelites), that they should not be troubled or deceived for it will take place after the beast or the antichrist has taken over Jerusalem and after the Great Tribulation.

As if that was not enough, let us also read what Daniel prophesied many years before Paul the Apostle was born, in Daniel 12:1

And at that time shall Michael stand up, the great prince, who standeth for the children of thy people, and there shall be a time of trouble, such as never was since there was a nation even to that same time; and at that time thy people shall be delivered; and every one that shall be found written in the book.

And at that time thy people and everyone that is found written in the book shall be delivered or raptured. What time? - The time of great trouble, such as never was; or as Jesus put it - the time of great tribulation, such as was not since the beginning of the world to this time (Matthew 24:21).

Immediately after Paul the Apostle taught the Thessalonians about the rapture in 1 Thessalonians chapter 4 verses 13 to 18, he went on to remind them about the timing also in chapter 5 verses 1 to 4 saying:

But of the times and the season, brethren, ye have no need that I write unto you. For yourselves know perfectly that the day of the Lord so cometh as a thief in the night. For when they say Peace and Safety, then sudden destruction cometh upon them, as travail upon a woman with child, and they shall not escape. But ye, brethren, are not in darkness, that that day should overtake you as a thief.

Paul clearly states here, to the disciples in Thessalonica, that the day of rapture will be as a thief in the night to the world and the unbelievers. But to the disciples, he said, but ye brethren, are not in darkness that that day should overtake you as a thief, because you are told of the timing and seasons which, of course, are explained in the pages of this book. Search the Scriptures very well; you will discover that everywhere that the rapture is mentioned, the timing and the season are also mentioned.

We are called to be wise, live in righteousness and be ready at all time so that when those days come, we shall be strong enough to do exploits prior to our final flight.

CHAPTER 4

Life After The Rapture: Part 1

The evacuation of the saints of God from the earth will be a historic experience; a fulfilment of the highly expected event. It will unfold joy in the life of the saints and sorrows for the unbelievers. This event will mark the end of our Christian pilgrimage on earth. The burden of tribulations and torture from the evil government will be over. Tears shall be wiped away and there shall be no more death, neither sorrows, nor crying, neither shall there be any more pains; for the old things shall pass away and behold all things shall become new. Imagine the flight without wings, the overcoming of the gravitational force; and the possessing of the body that cannot be destroyed. Certainly, Christians shall be changed and carried away for a life of joy without limitations.

The beginning of the life of celebration for Christ's followers will also mark the beginning of a life of torments and depression for the unbelievers. When Jesus appears, according to Revelation 11:18; the nations of the world shall mourn and cry for the period of vengeance of our God shall begin. The nations here are the unbelievers and the host of demons that fell with Lucifer. These fallen angels are the spirits that operate in most unbelievers, the antichrist and the false prophets. They are the same spirits that operated in the religious men, the Pharisees and the Sadducees that crucified Jesus on the cross. It was on this knowledge that David wrote in Psalms 2:1 and 2, saying;

Why do the nations rage and the people imagine a vain thing? The kings of the earth set themselves, and the rulers take council together, against the Lord, and against his anointed...

Jesus Christ also, while speaking with the scribes and the Pharisees said in John 8:40 and 44

But now ye seek to kill me, a man that hath told you the truth, which I have heard of God; this did not Abraham. Ye are of your father the devil, and the lust of your father ye will do. He was a murderer from the beginning, and abode not in the truth, because there is no truth in him. When he speaketh a lie, he speaketh of his own, for he is a liar and the father of it.

The evil that caused man to sin in the garden of Eden, which were later casted down as the fallen angels, are the same evil that tempted Jesus in the wilderness and later crucified him on the cross of Calvary. These fallen angels are in legions. Most of them operate through a non-regenerated heart and body of men and women. For example, they operated through the Pharisees to crucified Jesus Christ. Ordinary men would not love to kill the one who speaks the truth of salvation except the murderers who were in them. (John 8:44) The same evil angels are the accusers of the brethren today. These evil can operate through any man or woman who has not submitted his or her life to Jesus, for it is only in Jesus that their bondages and yokes are broken and are destroyed.

These rebellious fallen angels who are uncountable in number are the ones that operated in most empires of the world starting from the Babylonians to the Medo Persia, the Greece and the Roman Empire. Their aim has always been to oppose the name of God and afflict the people of the Most High God. They shall be the operators of the reform Roman Empire, which will include the government of the antichrist. (Revelation 13:2) At the appearing of Jesus, therefore, they shall be furious and shall rage with anger and they shall curse the name of the Most High God (Matthew 24:30, Revelation 11:18). They will rage because of the judgemental wrath that shall come upon them, namely the seven bowls of wrath of God and hell fire (Revelation 15:1-2 and Revelation 16:1-21).

And the angels who kept not their first estate, but left their own habitation, he has reserved in everlasting chains under darkness unto the judgement of the great day. Jude 6

Remember that these are the judgemental wraths that Christians shall not partake of, because they shall be poured out after the Rapture of the Saints. These plagues are not part of the Great Tribulation of the saints but the judgemental destruction of the unbelieving nations and those that shall receive the mark of the beast, his name or the number of his name.

Much more then, being now justified by his blood, we shall be saved from wrath through him. Romans 5:9

The Bible never mentioned that we shall be delivered before the Great Tribulation, rather from the wrath of God. That means that Christians who are alive in those days shall pass through the Great Tribulation but shall be raptured before the Judgemental wrath of God.

The Judgmental Wrath

And I saw another sign in heaven, great and marvellous, seven angels having the seven last plagues; for in them is filled up the wrath of God. And I saw, as it were a sea of glass mingled with fire, and them that hath gotten the victory over the beast, and over his image, and over his mark, and over the number of his name, standing on the sea of glass, having the harps of God. Revelation 15: 1 - 2

According to the above Scripture, Apostle John, on one hand, saw the angels with the bowls of wrath and, on the other hand, he saw the raptured saints who have won the victory over the beast. While the saints were celebrating the victory with harps, the angels of God were on the mission to torment the dwellers of the earth. To understand the details of the plagues that shall come upon the earth in those days, we shall study few verses in the book of Revelation chapter 16. There shall be seven plagues that shall come upon the earth one after the other.

And I heard a voice out of the temple saying to the seven angels, go your ways, and pour out the bowls of the wrath of God upon the earth. Revelation 16:1

The command to pour out the bowls of wrath upon the earth will be from God Almighty and the bowls of wrath shall involve the different epidemics, troubles or natural disasters that shall occur in different part of the world at different times. Some of the tribal strikes and killings or the outbreak of incurable diseases are the examples of the wrath of God upon the earth. The magnitude of these unusual happenings after the rapture shall be more terrible than what we have ever seen or heard of.

And the first went, and poured his bowl upon the earth, and there fell a foul and painful sore upon the men who had the mark of the beast and upon them who worshiped his image. Revelation 16:2

What shall happen in this time would be likened to what happened in the days of Moses when God sent him to Pharaoh to let Israel go, as recorded in the book of Exodus.

And the Lord said unto Moses and unto Aaron, take to you handfuls of ashes of the furnace, and let Moses sprinkle it toward heaven in the sight of Pharaoh. And it shall become small dust in all the land of Egypt, and shall be a boil breaking forth with ulcers upon man and upon beast. And the magicians could not stand before Moses because of the boils; for the boil was upon the magicians, and upon all the Egyptians. Exodus 9:8-11

The comparison of the wrath of sores as earlier read in Revelation 16:2 with the plagues of boils in Egypt is unique in many ways.

As Moses was told by God to throw the dust toward heaven for the commencement of the infliction of the boils upon the Egyptians, in the same way will the angel be commanded to pour the bowl of wrath upon the earth for the commencement of the sores upon the people of the earth.

The magicians could not cure or find a solution for the boils in Egypt; so also the sores upon the people of the earth shall be incurable, and the scientists and doctors shall have no answers. The plague of boils was a sudden outbreak, so also shall the wrath of sores be.

In the same manner, the second bowl of wrath of which turns the water of the sea to blood shall be poured by the second angel. Remember also that the water in Egypt was turned to blood as one of the plaques from God.

While the pains of the first and the second wrath of the judgment of God are still fresh, the third wrath shall be released, the fourth, the fifth, and the sixth (Revelation 16:4-16). In the sixth, the kings of the earth shall gather themselves in a place called Armageddon to fight against the Almighty.

And the sixth angel poured out his vial upon the great river Euphrates; and the water thereof was dried up, that the way of the kings of the east might be prepared. And I saw three unclean spirits like frogs come out of the mouth of the dragon, and out of the mouth of the beast, and out of the mouth of the false prophet. For they are the spirits of devils, working miracles, which go forth unto the kings of the earth and of the whole world, to gather them to the battle of that great day of God Almighty. Behold, I come as a thief. Blessed is he that watcheth, and keepeth his garments, lest he walk naked, and they see his shame. And he gathered them together into a place called in the Hebrew tongue Armageddon. Revelation 16:12-16

The effect of pain from the wrath of God shall cause the devil, the beast and the false prophet to release propaganda to draw together all the kings of the earth, religious leaders and the presidents of nations. Such propaganda is representative of the unclean spirits released as frogs in verse 13. These kings of the earth shall come together like the United Nation Security Council or United Nation Peace Conference or even as the Earth Summit in a place called Armageddon.

Armageddon is the ancient hill and valley of Megiddo, west of the Jordan in the plain of Jezreel, between Samaria and Galilee. The location is often referred to in the Old Testament as a military stronghold (2 Kings 9:27, 2 Kings 23:29 and Judges 5:19). This is the place that the beast will call the kings to gather to war against the Almighty and try to find solutions to the continuous wrath of God. And it shall be that when they have gathered, the seventh bowls of wrath shall be poured and hail shall fall out of heaven upon the dwellers of the earth.

And the seventh angel poured out his bowl into the air, and there come a great voice out of the temple of heaven, and from the throne saying, it is done. And there were voices and thunders, and lightning, and there was a great earthquake, such as was not since men were upon the earth, so mighty an earthquake, and so great. And there fell upon men a great hail out of heaven, every stone about the weight of a talent, and men blasphemed God because of the plague of the hail, for the plague was exceedingly great. Revelation 16:17, 18, 21

The terrible lightning and thunder shall cause fear and dismay, and men shall be slain. There shall be great torments upon the earth due to horrifying earthquakes and hailstones.

Reference could be made to the account of the seventh bowl of wrath in Exodus 9:13-26. What happened in Egypt was a test of what shall take place after the rapture.

Hell, the Lake of Fire

When the seventh bowl of wrath is poured upon the earth, the abomination of the devil and of the kings of the earth shall be remembered and they shall be rewarded in the fierceness of God's wrath.

And the great city was divided into three parts, and the cities of the nation shall fell; and great Babylon came in remembrance before God to give into her the cup of the wine of the fierceness of his wrath. Revelation 16:19

The crimes and abomination of the devil from the deception of Eve in Eden to the great tribulation of the saints shall be remembered by God, and the judgement for punishment and destruction shall be implemented. Every unrepented vessel used by the devil, her agents and supporters shall likewise be destroyed.

And I saw an angel standing in the sun; and he crieth with a loud voice, saying to all the fowls that fly in the midst of heaven, come and gather yourself together unto the supper of the great God. That ye may eat the flesh of kings, and the flesh of captains, and the flesh of mighty men, and the flesh of horses and of them that sit on them, and the flesh of all men both free and enslave both small and great. And I saw the beast, and the kings of the earth, and their armies, gathered together to make war against him that sat on the horse, and against his army. And the beast was taken, and with him the false prophet that wrought miracles before him with which he deceived them that had received the mark of the beast, and them that worship his image. These both were cast alive into a lake of fire burning with brimstone. And the remnants were slain with the sword of him that sat upon the horse, which sword proceeded out of his mouth; and all the fowls were filled with their flesh. Revelation 19:17-21

The above Scripture is generally referred to by many as the Battle of Armageddon. It is at this point that the Lord will destroy the agents of the devil. The kings, the captains, and the mighty men of this world who have made covenant with the devil because of greed for power, will all be destroyed in this battle. The operators of the last gentile rule; the beast, the false prophets, their supporters and their worshipers, shall be cast alive into the lake of fire, which is HELL. There shall they remain in torment for eternity. Also to be thrown in Hell are those that worshipped the beast and those that received his mark.

The people who live in sin shall be slain along with the antichrist and the false prophet. To avoid such terrible experience, such people are called to repentance and full submission to Jesus Christ, who is able to save and deliver all from sin and hell.

The Bottomless Pit

A careful study of the people that shall be destroyed, and those that shall be thrown into hell for the first time reveals that Satan, the devil will be excluded. The devil will be reserved for one last specific purpose. The purpose will be; to deceive the people that shall have evil intentions during the millennial reign of Christ and of the Saints. But the devil will not be left at ease; he shall be chained and thrown into the bottomless pit different from the lake of fire.

And I saw an angel come down from heaven having the key of the bottomless pit and a great chain in his hand. And he laid hold on the dragon, that old serpent, who is the Devil and Satan and bound him a thousand years. And cast him into the bottomless pit, and shut him up, and set a seal upon him, that he should deceive the nations no more, till the thousand years should be fulfilled; and after that he must be loosed a little season. Revelation 20:1-3

And it shall come to pass in that day, that the Lord shall punish the host of the high ones that are on high, and the kings of the earth upon the earth. And they shall be gathered together in the pit, and shall be shut up in the prison, and after many days shall they be visited. Isaiah 24:21-22

While the devil is shut up in detention, everyone that would be saved from hell and destrucion, would be obliged to worship and give glory to the Almighty God for the period of one thousand years. And after the one thousand years are completed, the devil shall be set at liberty to deceive the people again. Those whose hearts and intentions are wrong would be easily deceived.

They will join the devil to protest against the rulership of our God. But after a short while, the deceiver which is the devil and the men and women that would be deceived shall finally be destroyed in Hell - the lake of fire burning with brimstone.

And when the thousand years are ended, Satan shall be loosed out of the prison. He shall go out to deceive the nations which are in the four quarters of the earth, Gog and Magog, to gather them together to battle; the number of whom is as the sand of the sea. And they went up on the breadth of the earth, and compassed the camp of the saints about and the beloved city; and fire came down from God out of heaven, and devoured them. And the devil that deceived them was cast into the lake of fire and brimstone, where the beast and the false prophet are, and shall be tormented day and night forever and ever. Revelation 20:7-10

The devil will not be allowed to deceive the people for long because the government will not be given into his hands anymore. When he has gathered the people with deceptive hearts against the saints, the fire of God will descend to devour them. Then finally, the dragon, Satan, even that old devil, will be thrown into the lake of fire for eternal destruction.

In this chapter, I have explained the destruction of the heathen after the saints have been raptured and the destruction after the millennial reign of Christ. Let me also give some detail of the expectation of the believers in rapture.

CHAPTER 5

Life After The Rapture: Part 2

Again, many Christians are worried about where they shall be after the rapture; whether in heaven or on earth. Many are also worried about where the new heaven and new earth are. Let us find answers to some of these worries from the Scriptures.

1 Thessalonians 4:17 says, *Then we who are alive and remain shall be caught up together with them in the clouds to meet the Lord in the air and so shall we ever be with the Lord.*

Christian, who will be alive during the second coming of Christ, shall be raptured or transformed to meet with the resurrected saints in the cloud. Then both the resurrected and the transformed believers shall together meet the Lord in the air. The cloud will be a temporary meeting point where the saints, both the resurrected and the transformed shall meet as a congregation. Again, the air is another meeting place, where the congregation of saints shall meet with the Lord Jesus. Lastly, the second part of this verse declares; "and so shall we ever be with the Lord". Shall we be with the Lord in the cloud, or in the air, or in heaven? We shall ever be with the Lord wherever He goes. We shall live together with Him. He shall be our Shepherd, our King and our leader. Whether in the cloud, in the air, in heaven or on earth; we shall be together with Him.

For God hath not appointed us to wrath, but to obtain salvation by our Lord Jesus Christ. Who died for us that whether we wake or sleep, we should live together with him. 1 Thessalonians 5:9-10

We were appointed unto salvation through Jesus Christ that we will LIVE WITH HIM. Also Jesus while comforting the disciples before his crucifixion, told them in John 14:3

And if I go and prepare a place for you, I will come again and receive you unto myself, <u>that where I am; there ye may be also.</u>

So the question of where we shall be is hereby answered - WE SHALL BE WHERE HE WILL BE.

In Heaven or on Earth

And while they looked steadfastly toward heaven as he went up, behold two men stood by them in white apparel; who also said, ye men of Galilee, why stand ye gazing up into heaven? This same Jesus, who is taken up from you into heaven, shall so come in like manner as ye have seen him go into heaven. Acts 1:10-11

Jesus, the Son of God who was originally with the Father from creation came unto the earth to die and restore the dominion of man over the earth. On the completion of this divine assignment, he returned back to heaven to resume the position of authority. While His disciples stood on the Mount of Olives gazing into heaven during His ascension, two men (possibly, the angels of God) reminded them that this same Jesus shall return in a similar manner as He was taken up to heaven. In other words, Jesus shall come again to the earth. He has been received up into heaven and the next event is his second coming to the earth according to the Scriptures.

In what is commonly called the Lord's Prayer, Jesus taught the disciples to pray and say, *Thy kingdom come. Thy will be done on earth, as it is in heaven.* Matthew 6:10. The kingdom is already established in heaven, the same kingdom need to be restored on the earth as in the days of Adam and Eve before the temptation and fall of man. The restoration of this kingdom of heaven on the earth will be during the second coming of Jesus Christ.

There shall be a period of the millennial rule of Christ on earth, not in heaven. This millennial rule; that is the one thousand years of the rule of Christ with his saints has always been the expectation of the Jews - *the restoration of the kingdom to Israel.* This kingdom shall begin after the rapture and the destruction of the antichrist.

And I saw thrones, and they that sat upon them, and judgement was given unto them that were beheaded for the word of God and who had not worshiped the beast, neither received his mark upon their fore heads, or in their hands; and they lived and reigned with Christ a thousand years. Revelation 20:4

This refers to the raptured saints that they shall live and reign with Christ for one thousand years on earth, because the kingdom is to be established on earth. The kingdom will be heavenly in origin, principles and authority, but shall be set up on the earth with Jerusalem as the headquarters.

And it shall come to pass in the last days, that the mountain of the Lord's house shall be established in the top of the mountains, and shall be exalted above the hills; and all nations shall flow into it. And many people shall go and say, Come ye, and let us go to the mountain of the Lord, to the house of the God of Jacob; and he will teach us his ways, and we will walk in his paths; for out of Zion shall go forth the law and the word of God from Jerusalem. And he shall judge among the nations, and shall rebuke many peoples; and they shall beat their swords into ploughshares, and their spears into pruning hooks; nation shall not lift sword against nation, neither shall they learn war any more. Isaiah 2:2-4

The same vision that prophet Isaiah, the son of Amos, saw as recorded in Isaiah 2:1-4, was also revealed to prophet Micah, the Moreshethite, in Micah 4:1-5 about the same period of time in the 8th century B.C. God gave both men the same vision to prove the authenticity of the prophesy. The mountain of the Lord's house in these prophesies is the government of Christ, which shall be established over all other governments of this world.

This government shall be worldwide for many shall flow into it. And nations shall be judged in Jerusalem. As Rome was in the days of the Roman Empire, so shall Jerusalem be the Headquarters for the government of the whole world in the reign of Christ. All weapons of war shall be destroyed and nation shall not lift up sword against nation.

In the book of Matthew chapter 5 verses 3, 5 and 10; Jesus, in teaching about the kingdom to come, mentions the rewards for the faithful followers.

In verse 3, He says, *"Blessed are the poor in spirit for theirs is the kingdom of heaven."*

In verse 5, He says, *"Blessed are the meek; for they shall inherit the earth"*

And in verse 10, He says, *"Blessed are they who are persecuted for righteousness sake for theirs is the kingdom of heaven."*

Here, two kinds of reward are mentioned for three groups of faithful saints: the *kingdom of heaven* and *the inheritance of the earth*. But every good Christian that is *poor* in *spirit'* will be meek in character or behaviour. For being meek and humble, this Christian may also be *persecuted for righteousness sake*. For such a Christian, one may ask where his destiny will be - heaven or earth.

As earlier explained, the kingdom of heaven shall be established on earth at the coming of our Lord Jesus. Therefore, the possessors of the kingdom of heaven shall be the same people that shall inherit the earth and vice versa. This interpretation is according to the Scripture in this portion; but the choice of the reward for each Christian after the rapture is only determined by Christ, the Great Rewarder. Also, in the book of Daniel 7:27, the Bible say:

And the kingdom and dominion, and the greatness of the kingdom under the whole heaven, shall be given to the people of the saints of the Most High, whose kingdom is an everlasting kingdom, and all dominion shall serve and obey him.

The kingdom, which is heavenly, shall be established on earth but the dominion and the greatness of this kingdom shall be given to the saints.

You and I shall have dominion as priests and kings of the Most High. It is also important to know that some saints will have higher dominion than others depending on our faithfulness to God now.

And they sang a new song, saying, Thou art worthy to take the scroll, and to open its seals; for thou was slain and hast redeemed us to God by thy blood out of every kindred, and tongue and people and nation. And hast made us unto our God a Kingdom of priests, and we shall reign on the earth. Revelation 5:9-10

Again,

For the kingdom of heaven is as a man travelling into a far country: who called his own servants, and delivered unto them his goods. And unto one he gave five talents, to another two, and to another one; to every man according to his several ability: and straightway took his journey. Then he that had received the five talents went and traded with the same, and made them other five talents...
After a long time the lord of those servants cometh, and reckoneth with them. And so he that had received five talents came and brought other five talents, saying, Lord, thou deliveredst unto me five talents: behold, I have gained beside them five talents more. His lord said unto him, Well done, thou good and faithful servant: thou hast been faithful over a few things, I will make thee ruler over many things: enter thou into the joy of thy lord. Matthew 25:14-30

As laid out in chapter two of this book, one of the purposes of rapture is the provision of safety for the saints from destruction. Hence, the saints of God will be safely away from the scene of destruction on the earth. The saints will meet the Lord in the air and will continue with Him wherever He goes. The same saints will possess the earth for inheritance at the time deemed fit by the Lord himself.

CONCLUSION

Knowing that this life is not our final achievement and that there is a better life hereafter, what sort of people are we supposed to be? Eternity is eminent whether in condemnation or in redemption; you are bound to exist.

This book may have helped to clear some of your doubts about what shall take place in the last days. It has also given meaning to the hidden prophecies and teachings of the Scriptures that will help you understand the period in which we are now living. Remember, an accurate understanding of the events of the Endtime is a weapon that will help you do greater exploits even in the days of great tribulations.

And such as do wickedly against the covenant shall he corrupt by flatteries; but the people that do know their God shall be strong and do exploits. And they that understand among the people shall instruct many; yet they shall fall by the sword; and by spoil many days. Daniel 11:32-33

The knowledge of what is intended in the last days is a great weapon against the flatteries of the world and that of the antichrist in particular. According to verse 33 of Daniel 11, when the love of many waxes cold, a man of understanding will be able to instruct and encourage his household, his local congregation, his friends and as many that will be attentive to him. He will instruct them of the divine purpose of God and of the duration of time. Above all, he will encourage them with the victory and rewards for those that shall endure unto the end.

To those who are not sure of their relationship with Christ, may the knowledge acquired through this book prompt you to give God a chance in your life in order to avoid the coming frustration and destruction. Let nothing keep you in bondage against the decision of your liberty; not even the cares of this life nor the love of this world.

According as his divine power hath given unto us all things that pertain to life and Godliness, through the Knowledge of him that hath called us to glory and virtue. 2 Peter 1:3

Through the knowledge of Christ, God has already provided for every situation of life that comes or will ever come our ways. As Paul will say, nay, in all these things we are more than conquerors through Christ that loved us. Romans 8:37. As believers, we will have to train our flesh to obey and love the things of God. Since the flesh will not inherit the kingdom of God, we do not have to walk according to its lusts.

Now the works of the flesh are manifest, which are these: adultery, fornication, uncleanness, lasciviousness, idolatry, sorcery, hatred, strife, jealousy, wrath, factions, seditions, heresies, envying, murders, drunkenness, revelling, and the like; of which I told you before, as I have also told you in time past, that they who do such things shall not inherit the kingdom of God. Galatians 5:19-21

The flesh loves to do these things, but these things can stop us from the victory prepared for us. Therefore, we have to stop them before they stop us, and it is only in Christ Jesus that the flesh can be controlled. Accept Christ today and avoid the impending frustration and torment. Visit a living Pentecostal Church and accept Christ into your life. He is waiting.

In the other hand, if you have been in Church, but not sure of your relationship with Christ, check your life again. If you should die today, where will you be - with the redeemed or with the condemned? There is no change of mind in the grave. Be bold today to make an outstanding decision for holiness in Christ.

If you have made this decision, then pray this prayer with me;

Lord Jesus,
I faithfully accept you this day as my Lord and Saviour.
I repent of my sins and mistakes.
I surrender my life to you in obedience to your word.
Help me to serve you in holiness so that I will be with you at your coming.
Thank you my Father in heaven for accepting me as your son / daughter.
This I pray in the name of Jesus Christ,
Amen.

Dear friends, it is not enough just to go to Church services but it is important to belong to a spirit-filled Church that teaches the truth with the wisdom of God; and the knowledge of His Word shall keep you until He comes.

MARANATHA!
OUR LORD COMES!
AMEN.

WE CAN HELP YOU TO GROW SPIRITUALLY

Do you have any question or do you need spiritual help?
Write or email us today and we shall attend to you with all urgency.
Your spiritual growth is important to us.

Mega life Network
New Life Covenant Church
Eiswerder Str, 18 (Haus 130)
13585 Berlin, Germany
+49 (30) 23136818
info@newlife-international.com
www.newlife-international.com

www.ingramcontent.com/pod-product-compliance
Lightning Source LLC
Chambersburg PA
CBHW071541080526
44588CB00011B/1744